LSU TIGERS

BY K.C. KELLEY

Published by The Child's World®
1980 Lookout Drive • Mankato, MN 56003-1705
800-599-READ • www.childsworld.com

Copyright ©2022 by The Child's World®
All rights reserved. No part of this book may be reproduced or utilized in any form or by any means without written permission from the publisher.

Cover and 2: Gerald Herbert/AP Images.
Interior: AP Images: Alex Brandon 8; 19; Dreamstime: Mfmegevand 12; Newscom: Todd Kirkland/Icon Sportswire 15, 16; Jeffrey Vest/Icon SMI 20. Shutterstock: Arcorn 4. Wikimedia: 7 (2); 11 (2).

ISBN 9781503850330 (Reinforced Library Binding)
ISBN 9781503850583 (Portable Document Format)
ISBN 9781503851344 (Online Multi-user eBook)
LCCN: 2021930299

Printed in the United States of America

Touchdown! Time for the LSU Tigers to celebrate.

CONTENTS

Why We Love College Football 4

CHAPTER ONE
Early Days 6

CHAPTER TWO
Glory Years 9

CHAPTER THREE
Best Year Ever! 10

CHAPTER FOUR
LSU Traditions 13

CHAPTER FIVE
Meet the Mascot 14

CHAPTER SIX
Top LSU QBs 17

CHAPTER SEVEN
Other LSU Heroes 18

CHAPTER EIGHT
Recent Superstars 21

Glossary 22

Find Out More 23

Index 24

WHY WE LOVE COLLEGE FOOTBALL

The leaves are changing color. Happy crowds fill the stadiums. Pennants wave. And here come the fight songs. It's time for college football! The sport is one of America's most popular. Millions of fans follow their favorite teams. They wear school colors and hope for big wins.

Louisiana State University, known as LSU, is one of the top teams in the country. The team's fans are loud and loyal. They cheer for the purple-and-gold to win every game. Let's meet the LSU Tigers!

Another night for LSU football in front of a packed house.

CHAPTER ONE

Early Days

LSU started playing football in 1894. They were very good right away. The school's first perfect season was in 1895. Four of the next 13 seasons were perfect.

A big star in 1908 was Doc Fenton. Most games did not see many points in those days. Football was a lot rougher. Fenton stood out when he scored 125 points by himself in LSU's 10 wins that season.

WHY TIGERS?

LSU teams have been called Tigers since 1896. The nickname comes from a group of **Confederate** soldiers from Louisiana. They fought fiercely in the Civil War (1861–65).

Above: The 1898 LSU team shows off its team sweaters and padded pants.

Right: Doc Fenton was one of the school's first football heroes. He starred on the 1908 team.

LSU
TIGERS

CHAPTER TWO

Glory Years

In 1935, LSU won its first Southeastern **Conference** (SEC) title. The next year, the Tigers went 9-1-1 (wins-losses-ties). They were ranked number two in the country!

The 1946 team lost only one game. They played in the Cotton Bowl against Arkansas. Ice, sleet, and snow poured down on both teams. Fans shivered in the stands! The "Ice Bowl" ended in a 0-0 tie!

The 1961 team lost its first game of the season. Then it won ten in a row! The last was a big win in the Orange Bowl.

Nick Saban took over as coach in 2000. In 2003, he led the Tigers to their first national title since 1958. LSU were champs again in 2007 with coach Les Miles.

◄ *Quarterback Ryan Perrilloux shows off his leaping ability. He was part of the Tigers' 2007 national championship team.*

CHAPTER THREE

Best Year Ever!

Defense led the way when LSU won the 1958 national title. The team allowed more than ten points in only one game. They had four **shutouts**.

Coach Paul Dietzel ran his team in a new way. Usually, players go in and out one at a time. Dietzel swapped in whole groups. The defense changed each play. That kept players fresh all game long.

In the Sugar Bowl, LSU beat Clemson 7–0. The LSU Tigers were tops! It was their first team with a perfect record since 1908!

> **THE STAR**
> Billy Cannon played **halfback** for the 1958 team. He ran and passed for touchdowns. His great speed made him hard to stop. Cannon even kicked extra points! He was the SEC's Most Valuable Player (MVP). Dietzel said Cannon was "the finest football player I ever coached."

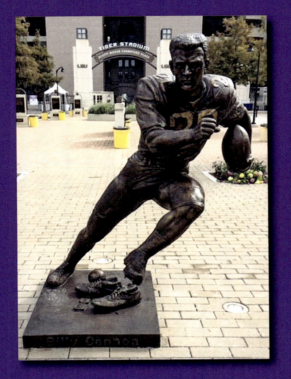

LSU
TIGERS

Billy Cannon in metal and in real life.

Dressed in purple and gold, LSU fans stream into Tiger Stadium for another big game.

CHAPTER FOUR

LSU Traditions

Every school has football traditions. Some are fun for the fans. Others are part of playing for the team. Here are a few LSU football traditions:

Geaux Tigers: Many people in Louisiana speak French. This cheer rhymes a made-up French word with "Go."

Victory Hill Walk: The LSU band plays before the game on this campus spot. Then the football team marches down the hill. Fans cheer as their heroes head to the stadium.

Crossbar: Players touch a piece of the crossbar as they run onto the field. The metal pole was on the field until the 1950s.

Night Games: Since 1931, most LSU home games are at night. It must work. The Tigers win more games when they play at night.

CHAPTER FIVE

Meet the Mascot

LSU has two types of tiger **mascots**.

Mike the Tiger is a live tiger. He lives in a special home near the stadium. A small cage is rolled onto the field before each game. Mike roars along with the fans! The first Mike was born in 1936. The newest Mike was born in 2018.

During games, a student dresses up as Mike, too. He dances around and helps fans cheer. The costumed Mike also goes to other LSU sports events.

LOUD!
LSU fans are known as some of the loudest in the nation. In a 1988 game, LSU scored to beat Auburn. The fans cheered so loudly that machines at the school measured the ground **vibrating** under the stadium!

While the real Mike the Tiger stays in a cage, a costumed Mike cheers with fans.

CHAPTER SIX

Top LSU QBs

Quarterback is the most important position in football. LSU has had its share of great QBs.

Y.A. Tittle led the Tigers in 1945 and 1946. Years later, he became a **Hall of Fame** QB in the NFL.

Another future NFL star was Bert Jones. He was the LSU QB from 1970 to 1972. He was named All-SEC and led the Tigers to three bowl games.

No QB won more games for LSU than Tommy Hodson. His 9,115 passing yards are an LSU all-time record.

In 2019, QB Joe Burrow had one of the best college seasons ever. He won the Heisman Trophy. He had five TD passes in the national championship game. LSU beat Clemson 42–25.

← Joe Burrow threw 60 TD passes in 2019, the most ever in a single season by a college quarterback.

CHAPTER SEVEN

Other LSU Heroes

When Gaynell Tinsley was at LSU, players did it all. From 1935 to 1937, Tinsley was a star receiver. He also played defensive end! He was named a member of the **All-America** team.

Jim Taylor was the top scorer in the country in 1957. He had 86 points for LSU and was a member of the All-America team. He felt right at home. Taylor was born in Baton Rouge, where LSU is!

> **LSU HEISMAN TROPHY WINNERS**
> This award goes to the best player in college football. Tigers have won it twice.
> • Billy Cannon, 1958
> • Joe Burrow, 2019

From 1969 to 1971, Tommy Casanova was LSU's only three-time member of the All-America team. Casanova played defense and returned kicks. He also played running back. He is one of 10 LSU players in the College Football Hall of Fame.

Tommy Casanova (37) takes to the air to fly past a tackler. Casanova was an all-around star for three seasons.

CHAPTER EIGHT

Recent Superstars

Andrew Whitworth is one of the best **offensive linemen** in the NFL. Before that, he starred at LSU. He started 52 games. That's the second most ever. In 2003, he helped LSU win the national title.

Defensive back Tyrann Mathieu had a great nickname. He was called "The Honey Badger." He was as fierce as one of those mammals! Patrick Peterson was another star on defense. He was a two-time member of the All-America team. He covered receivers like glue and was also a star punt returner.

Odell Beckham Jr. is one of the NFL's most exciting receivers. He got his start at LSU as an all-around star. He caught TD passes, but also returned punts and kicks.

What players on today's LSU Tigers will become all-time stars?

Odell Beckham Jr. was following a family tradition. Both of his parents were athletes at LSU.

GLOSSARY

All-America (ALL uh-MAYR-ih-kuh) an honor given to the top players in college sports

Confederate (kon-FED-er-ut) the group of states that broke away from the United States during the Civil War

conference (KON-fur-enss) a group of schools that plays sports against each other

halfback (HAFF-bak) an offensive position that runs with the football and catches passes

Hall of Fame (HALL UV FAYM) a list or a place that honors the greatest players in a sport

mascots (MASS-kots) costumed characters that help fans cheer

offensive linemen (AW-fenss-iv LYN-men) players who block for the quarterback and running backs

shutouts (SHUT-owts) games in which no points are allowed by one team

vibrating (VY-brayt-ing) moving back and forth very rapidly

FIND OUT MORE

IN THE LIBRARY

Football: Then to WOW! New York:
Sports Illustrated Kids, 2014.

Jacobs, Greg. *The Everything Kids' Football Book*. New York: Adams Media, 2018.

Miller, Tessa. *LSU Tigers*. New York: Weigl, 2020.

ON THE WEB

Visit our website for links about the
LSU Tigers:
childsworld.com/links

Note to Parents, Teachers, and Librarians: We routinely verify our Web links to make
sure they are safe and active sites. So encourage your readers to check them out!

INDEX

Arkansas, 9
Auburn, 14
Beckham, Odell Jr., 21
Burrow, Joe, 2, 17, 18
Cannon, Billy, 10, 11, 18
Casanova, Tommy, 18
Civil War, 6
Clemson, 10, 17
Dietzel, Pau, 10
Fenton, Doc, 6, 7
Heisman Trophy, 10, 17, 18
Hodson, Tommy, 17
Ice Bowl, 9
Jones, Bert, 17
Mathieu, Tyrann, 21

Mike the Tiger, 14
Miles, Les, 9
Perrilloux, Ryan, 9
Peterson, Patrick, 21
Saban, Nick, 9
Southeastern Conference
    (SEC), 9, 10, 17
Sugar Bowl, 10
Taylor, Jim, 18
Tiger Stadium, 12, 13
Tittle, Y.A., 17
Tinsley, Gaynell, 18
Victory Hill Walk, 13
Whitworth, Andrew, 21

ABOUT THE AUTHOR

K.C. Kelley is the author of more than
100 sports books for young readers, including
numerous biographies of famous athletes. He went
to the University of California—Berkeley, but his
Golden Bears didn't quite make it into this series!